KENNY JOHNSON

Fathers Matter

KLP

KINGDOM LEGACY
PRESS

To my grandfathers, who laid the foundation.

To my father, who showed me strength and discipline.

*To my children, who inspire me to be the best version of myself
every day.*

*May this book serve as a guide for generations to come, honoring
the role of fathers as God intended.*

*"And I will be your Father, and you will be my sons and daughters,
says the Lord Almighty." – 2 Corinthians 6:18 (NLT)*

Contents

Preface

The Sacred Name: Yahshua (Jesus)

Throughout this book, you will notice the name Yahshua (Jesus) used consistently in every prayer, scripture, and spiritual reference. This is not by accident. It is a divine restoration—an invitation to deeper understanding and reverence for the One who came to save.

1. Yahshua: The Original Name of the Messiah

Before Greek, Latin, or English translations existed, the Son of God was called by His Hebrew name: Yahshua (יהושוע), meaning "Yah is salvation" or "Yahweh saves." This name embodies His mission and identity—not only as Savior but as the fulfillment of the Father's promise.

"She will give birth to a son, and you are to give Him the name Yahshua, because He will save His people from their sins."
   (Matthew 1:21, Hebrew Roots Translation)

In most Bibles, this verse uses the name Jesus, but in the original tongue, Yahshua was the name given. His name connects to the divine name of the Father—Yahweh—revealing the unity between Father and Son.

"I have come in My Father's name, and you do not receive Me."
   (John 5:43)

"Your name, O YHWH, endures forever, Your renown, O YHWH, through all generations."
   (Psalm 135:13)

The very name Yahshua carries that same eternal Name—Yah—which is lost in the Greek and English forms.

2. Jesus: The Translated Name with Continued Grace

The name "Jesus" came into popular usage through a series of linguistic transitions:

Hebrew "Yahshua"

Greek "Iēsous" (Greek lacks the "Y" and "sh" sounds)

Latin "Iesus"

English "Jesus" (with the letter "J" being introduced around the 16th century)

Although the name "Jesus" is not linguistically the same as "Yahshua," it carries spiritual power because of the faith and reverence placed in it by generations of believers. God responds to the heart, not merely phonetics.

"There is no other name under heaven given among men by which we must be saved."

(Acts 4:12)

"For whoever calls on the name of the Lord shall be saved."
   (Romans 10:13)

These verses affirm the saving power of the name, even when pronounced differently, so long as the heart is aligned in truth and faith.

3. Reclaiming the Power of the Name

In these last days, the Father is restoring lost truths—identities, cultures, and languages that were stripped through colonization, translation, and assimilation. Reclaiming the name Yahshua is not to dismiss or diminish the name "Jesus," but to honor the original and reveal the fullness of His identity.

"The name of YHWH is a strong tower; the righteous run to it and are safe."
   (Proverbs 18:10)

"Then I will restore to the peoples a pure language, that they all may call on the name of YHWH, to serve Him with one accord."
   (Zephaniah 3:9)

The enemy has always sought to distort identity and language, because names carry power, assignment, and spiritual authority. The restoration of Yahshua's name is part of the greater awakening happening among God's people.

4. How This Book Will Use His Name

To walk in both truth and accessibility, this book will use Yahshua (Jesus) throughout—bridging the gap between what has been passed down and what is being restored.

"Yahshua the Messiah is the same yesterday, today, and forever."
  (Hebrews 13:8, Hebrew Roots Bible)

Every prayer, every scripture, and every reflection is written to honor both the faith many were raised with and the deeper truth now being revealed. Let this understanding open your spirit to greater revelation. May you call on Him, not out of tradition, but with truth and intimacy. Whether you say Jesus or Yahshua, may your prayers be filled with power, and your walk be filled with light.

"And you shall know the truth, and the truth shall make you free."
  (John 8:32)

Introduction

The Call to Fatherhood

The irony of what has led me to write this book is the very shirt I am wearing right now—"Fathers Matter." My wife originally bought this shirt for me, and the first time I wore it was on our trip to Gatlinburg, Tennessee. As an African-American father in a predominantly different environment, I was stopped nearly every other block—not out of suspicion, but out of respect, gratitude, and admiration. Men and women, young and old, expressed appreciation for the message, acknowledging the reality that fatherhood is under attack, yet deeply valued.

Specifically, in African-American and minority homes, we have been systematically driven out—by both external forces and, at times, by our own shortcomings. This strategic removal has contributed to the collapse of families, communities, and ultimately society as a whole. Recognizing this, the Lord has pressed upon my heart to write this book, not just for one demographic, but for all fathers—current and future. This book is a call to action for every man who has been entrusted with the gift of fatherhood. Whether you are raising your children in the home, navigating co-parenting, or stepping into the role of a mentor or father figure, your role is divine.

"Fathers, do not provoke your children to anger by the way you treat them. Rather, bring them up with the discipline and instruction that comes from the Lord." – Ephesians 6:4 (NLT)

My First Experience with Fatherhood

In the summer of 2019, God blessed me with my firstborn son, Ezra. At the time, I did not feel fully prepared. I felt overwhelmed, questioning my ability to be the father he needed. I even wrestled with doubts about his authenticity as my biological child due to past premarital relationships. But despite the uncertainty, God gave me peace in my spirit—I knew he was mine. Ezra was born prematurely and spent a month and a half in the NICU. Every single day, I was there reading to him, speaking life over him, and praying for him. I watched him grow stronger, gain weight, and overcome challenges. And when the moment finally arrived—the first time I could hold my son in my arms—it was as if time stood still. I held him against my bare chest, and in that moment, we became unified as father and son. This experience changed me forever. It made me fully comprehend the depth of a father's love. And in doing so, I also began to grasp the immeasurable love that our Heavenly Father has for us.

"See how very much our Father loves us, for he calls us his children, and that is what we are!" – 1 John 3:1 (NLT)

The Struggles Fathers Face

In the early years of fatherhood, I struggled to balance work, faith, and family. I felt like I never had enough time for my children. I felt like I wasn't doing enough as a father. I felt like I was failing. But looking back, I realize now that time was never the issue—it was my priorities. Time is a man-made construct, but what we do with our time determines everything. I had to learn that being a father wasn't about providing just financial support—it was about providing spiritual, emotional, and physical presence. When I became intentional as a father, I immediately saw the shift. My children became more secure, more confident, and more joyful. As I aligned myself with God, He was able to flow through me to my children.

Fathers Must Take Responsibility

Fatherhood is the greatest honor a man can receive. But it is also the most difficult responsibility. As men, we must take accountability for the state of fatherhood in today's world. We have compromised—giving in to the temptations and distractions that pull us away from our families. We have neglected our spiritual authority. And because of this, our children are suffering. But it doesn't have to be this way. We can rise up. We can align with God's divine order. We can reclaim our role as fathers, protectors, and leaders.

"The father of godly children has cause for joy. What a pleasure to have children who are wise." – Proverbs 23:24 (NLT)

Repenting and Restoring Fatherhood

When I fully surrendered to God, I sat my children down in front of my wife and apologized to them. I apologized for the moments I wasn't fully present. I asked for their forgiveness. Tears streamed down my face as I realized that I had been physically there but not always mentally or spiritually present. My children accepted my apology, and from that moment forward, I vowed to never take fatherhood lightly again. Since then, I have made it my mission to start every morning covering my family in prayer, covering my children in prayer, and covering myself in prayer—so that I may be everything God has called me to be.

"But if we confess our sins to him, he is faithful and just to forgive us our sins and to cleanse us from all wickedness." – 1 John 1:9 (NLT)

A Call to All Fathers – Rise Up!

Now, the Lord is calling you to step into your divine role. This book is not just another book on fatherhood—it is a movement. It is a wake-up call for every father to rise up, take a stand, and become all that God has destined him to be. If you are a father, you have been chosen. If you are a father, you are a leader. If you are a father, you are the protector of your home and the first spiritual covering over your children. This is a declaration—for all fathers, future fathers, and father figures—to walk boldly in their calling. The children of God are not for sale. The next generation belongs to the Lord. Let's rise up. Let's bring our children back to God, just as He has called us to do.

"Then Yahshua (Jesus) called for the children and said to the disciples, "Let the children come to me. Don't stop them! For the Kingdom of God belongs to those who are like these children.." – Luke 18:16 (NLT)

1

Chapter 1: The History and Decline of Fatherhood

The War on Fatherhood is a Spiritual Battle

The decline of fatherhood is not just a societal problem—it is a spiritual attack on the role God ordained for men. Fathers are called to be leaders, protectors, and providers, but many have unknowingly surrendered their role due to the corruption of the seven deadly sins. These sins have infiltrated the lives of men, weakening fathers spiritually, mentally, emotionally, and physically. Each one is a weapon the enemy uses to keep men from stepping fully into their divine calling and from leading their families with strength and wisdom. "For we are not fighting against flesh-and-blood enemies, but against evil rulers and authorities of the unseen world, against mighty powers in this dark world, and against evil spirits in the heavenly places." – Ephesians 6:12 (NLT) As I reflect on my own journey, I recognize that I was plagued with all seven deadly sins at different points in my life. These sins negatively impacted my relationship with God, my wife, my children, and even myself. But God is merciful, and through humility, discipline, and His unwavering love, I have broken free. This chapter is an honest look at how these sins destroy fathers—and how we can overcome them through faith, wisdom, and intentional action.

1. Pride – The Silent Killer of the Righteous Father

Pride is the foundation of destruction. It blinds men from seeking wisdom, admitting faults, and growing spiritually. Pride makes a father believe he must do everything alone. Pride keeps men from asking for help or accepting correction. Pride can manifest as either arrogance or victimhood. For me, pride was a double-edged sword. At times, it made me egotistical, thinking I was always right and never wrong. Other times, it would trap me in a victim mentality, making me blame others instead of taking accountability for my own actions. This pride weakened my relationships—especially with my family and God. It was through the wisdom of God-centered men, pastors, and my own father that I began to recognize the damage pride had caused. "My child, don't reject the Lord's discipline, and don't be upset when he corrects you. For the Lord corrects those he loves, just as a father corrects a child in whom he delights." – Proverbs 3:11-12 (NLT)

Overcoming Pride:
Seek wisdom from godly men and mentors.
Embrace correction as a path to growth, not an attack.
Recognize that fatherhood is not meant to be done alone.

2. Lust – The Unseen Distraction That Steals Fatherhood

Lust is one of the most destructive sins for men because it distorts the mind, pollutes the heart, and pulls men away from their families. Lust turns a father's focus from his family to fleeting temptations. Lust is a gateway to broken trust, addiction, and distraction. Lust is everywhere—social media, entertainment, clothing trends, and culture. Lust was a battle for me that took deep prayer, fasting, and discipline to conquer. I remember being out with my family, and yet my mind would wander, my eyes would stray. This act is often referred to as rubbernecking—when a man habitually turns his head to look at another woman, even when he's with his wife or family. Yahshua (Jesus) was clear about lust: it begins in the eyes before it ever reaches the flesh. "But I say, anyone who even looks at a woman with lust has already committed adultery with her in his heart." – Matthew 5:28 (NLT)

Overcoming Lust:
    Guard your eyes and your heart—avoid triggers.
    Fast and pray to break the cycle of lustful thoughts.
    Replace lust with love, temperance, and self-control.

3. Greed – The Pursuit of Success Over Fatherhood

Greed is deceptive—it makes men believe that financial success equals success in fatherhood. Greed leads men to chase money more than they chase their children. Greed makes fathers prioritize wealth over time and presence. Greed leads to burnout, discontentment, and broken priorities. I was once so focused on creating generational wealth that I became consumed with business opportunities, investments, and financial growth. My focus was on making money faster, rather than making memories with my children. There's a saying: "Quick money in is quick money out." The correct quote is: "Wealth from get-rich-quick schemes quickly disappears; wealth from hard work grows over time." – Proverbs 13:11 (NLT)

Overcoming Greed:
   Focus on what truly lasts—your legacy, not just wealth.
   Prioritize time with your children over financial gain.
   Trust that God will provide when you align with His will.

4. Sloth – The Passive Fatherhood Trap

Sloth isn't just laziness—it's spiritual passivity. Sloth makes men passive instead of intentional. Sloth keeps fathers from leading their homes. Sloth leads to procrastination and un-fulfilled responsibilities. I once believed that if I just prayed, manifested, and meditated, God would bring things to me. But faith without works is dead. "Never be lazy, but work hard and serve the Lord enthusiastically." – Romans 12:11 (NLT)

Overcoming Sloth:
   Take action daily—prayer must be followed by movement.
   Lead your home with intention, not passivity.
   Recognize that God rewards diligence and effort.

5. Wrath – The Unchecked Anger That Destroys Homes

Anger is often generational—it is passed down through fathers who never learned to control it. Wrath damages relationships and causes resentment. Wrath turns discipline into destruction. Wrath creates generational trauma. I have had to constantly work on my patience and balance in discipline. The Bible says: "Fathers, do not provoke your children to anger by the way you treat them. Rather, bring them up with the discipline and instruction that comes from the Lord." – Ephesians 6:4 (NLT)

Overcoming Wrath:
Pause before reacting—pray for patience.
Discipline with love, not frustration.
Teach, guide, and uplift your children rather than break their spirits.

6. Envy – The Thief of Gratitude

Envy makes men compare themselves to others instead of embracing their own blessings. Comparison steals joy. Envy makes men resent their own journey. Gratitude is the antidote to envy. "A peaceful heart leads to a healthy body; jealousy is like cancer in the bones." – Proverbs 14:30 (NLT)

Overcoming Envy:
Celebrate what God has given you.
Practice daily gratitude.
Sharpen other men rather than compete with them.

"As iron sharpens iron, so a friend sharpens a friend." – Proverbs 27:17 (NLT)

7. Gluttony – The Overindulgence That Weakens Fathers

Gluttony isn't just about food—it's about excess in all things. Gluttony leads to unhealthy habits that affect fatherhood. Gluttony makes men undisciplined. Gluttony must be replaced with self-control. "A person without self-control is like a city with broken-down walls." – Proverbs 25:28 (NLT)

Overcoming Gluttony:
Lead by example—practice self-discipline.
Eliminate distractions and unnecessary indulgences.
Show your children what true health looks like.

Chapter 2: The Crisis of Fatherhood – The Decline and the Path to Restoration

The Silent Crisis in Fatherhood

The seven deadly sins have weakened fathers at their core, leading to broken homes, absent leadership, and spiritual disconnection. As we examined in Chapter 1, these sins have stripped men of their divine calling, making fatherhood more difficult and less prioritized in modern society. But these sins are not just personal struggles—they have been weaponized against us. Over the last century, fatherhood has been systematically attacked and devalued, leaving generations of children without the guidance, protection, and leadership of a present and engaged father. This crisis is not a natural progression of society—it is intentional. We must recognize the historical strength of fatherhood, the deliberate dismantling of the father's role, and what the numbers reveal about the devastating consequences of fatherlessness. Most importantly, we must understand how to restore fatherhood to its rightful place in the family and society. "The godly walk with integrity; blessed are their children who follow them." – Proverbs 20:7 (NLT)

The Strength of Fatherhood Throughout History

For thousands of years, fatherhood was the backbone of civiliza-
tion. Strong fathers built strong families, and strong families
built thriving communities. In biblical times, fathers were
responsible for their children's spiritual leadership. In ancient
societies, men led, protected, and provided for their homes with
honor. Up until recent history, fathers were the undisputed
head of the household, shaping the next generation's morals,
discipline, and faith. "Direct your children onto the right path,
and when they are older, they will not leave it." – Proverbs
22:6 (NLT) From Abraham, Isaac, and Jacob to the founding
fathers of nations, the role of the father was considered a
divine responsibility. Fathers in early civilizations passed down
wisdom, wealth, and discipline. Fatherhood was seen as an
honor, not a burden. A man's legacy was determined by the
strength and character of his children. So what changed?
How did we go from strong, engaged fathers to a world where
fatherhood is dismissed, mocked, and even demonized?

The Systematic Attack on Fathers

The decline of fatherhood was not an accident. It was orches-
trated through historical events, policy changes, and cultural
shifts that made it increasingly difficult for fathers to stay
in their children's lives. The Industrial Revolution (1800s-
1900s): Fathers were pulled away from the home for long work
hours, weakening their role in raising children. Welfare Policies
(1960s-1970s): Government assistance programs penalized

father involvement, leading to an increase in single-mother households. The Sexual Revolution & No-Fault Divorce (1970s-Present): Marriage became less stable, and fathers became more easily removed from their children's lives. Cultural Shifts in Media (1980s-Present): Television, movies, and advertising began to mock and devalue fathers, portraying them as idiots, weaklings, or unnecessary. "The thief's purpose is to steal and kill and destroy. My purpose is to give them a rich and satisfying life." – John 10:10 (NLT) By the time the 21st century arrived, fatherhood was no longer viewed as essential—it became optional. And as a result, we have seen the greatest crisis of fatherlessness in human history.

The Current Crisis: What the Numbers Say

The absence of fathers has led to devastating consequences. 85% of youths in prison grew up in fatherless homes (U.S. Department of Justice). 71% of high school dropouts come from homes without fathers (National Principals Association Report). Children without fathers are 4X more likely to live in poverty (U.S. Census Bureau). Teen pregnancies and early sexual activity are significantly higher in father-absent homes. Children with absent fathers are more likely to struggle with depression, anxiety, and suicidal thoughts (American Academy of Pediatrics). "Children are a gift from the Lord; they are a reward from him." – Psalm 127:3 (NLT) This is not just a coincidence—it is the direct result of the deconstruction of fatherhood. And just when fathers were beginning to recognize the crisis and fight back, a new attack emerged—the Digital Revolution.

The Digital Revolution – A New Attack on Fathers

The Industrial Revolution pulled fathers away from the home physically, but the Digital Revolution has pulled fathers away mentally, emotionally, and spiritually. The average adult spends over 7 hours a day on screens (Statista, 2023). Social media addiction leads to increased anxiety, depression, and distraction (Journal of Behavioral Addictions). Many fathers spend more time on their phones than engaging with their children. I was guilty of this. I remember times when I was physically present with my children, but mentally absent—scrolling through my phone, distracted by social media. Then one day, my phone broke unexpectedly. What initially frustrated me turned into a blessing. Without my phone, I was suddenly more engaged, more present, and more connected to my family. "So be careful how you live. Don't live like fools, but like those who are wise. Make the most of every opportunity in these evil days." – Ephesians 5:15-16 (NLT) The enemy wants to distract fathers— because a distracted father is an ineffective father.

Restoring Fatherhood – The Path Forward

We cannot afford to let another generation be raised without strong, present, and engaged fathers. We must reject society's attempt to weaken fatherhood. We must resist the temptations that pull us away from our families. We must be intentional, present, and engaged with our children.

1. Reclaim Spiritual Leadership in the Home

Lead your children in prayer, Bible study, and worship. Teach them godly values and biblical principles. Be their first example of what a man of God looks like. "But as for me and my family, we will serve the Lord." – Joshua 24:15 (NLT)

2. Prioritize Presence Over Provision

Time is the most valuable gift you can give your children. Put the phone down, be present, and engage with them daily. Money and success mean nothing if your children don't know you. "Teach us to realize the brevity of life, so that we may grow in wisdom." – Psalm 90:12 (NLT)

3. Build a Brotherhood of Fathers

Surround yourself with godly men who sharpen you. Encourage and uplift other fathers in your community. Be a mentor to fatherless young men who need guidance. "Listen to counsel and accept discipline, that you may be wise in your latter days." – Proverbs 19:20 (NLT)

Final Call to Action: Fathers, It's Time to Rise Up

The enemy has worked tirelessly to destroy fatherhood—but we will not allow it to continue. We must stand firm, fight back, and restore fatherhood in our homes, communities, and the world. Your children need you. Your family needs you. The world needs you. The time to act is now. "I will be his father, and he will be my son. If he sins, I will correct and discipline him with the rod, like any father would do." – 2 Samuel 7:14 (NLT)

3

Chapter 3: A Father's Presence – Why Being There Matters

The Power of a Present Father

Fatherhood is more than just a title, it is an active role, a calling, and a divine responsibility. A father's presence in the home directly shapes a child's emotional security, confidence, and future success. A present father strengthens his children's identity. A present father teaches discipline, responsibility, and love. A present father provides spiritual, emotional, and mental guidance. But in today's world, many fathers are physically present but mentally and emotionally absent. Others have been removed from their children's lives by divorce, separation, or systematic obstacles. Regardless of the situation, the absence of a father leaves a void that no government program, mentor, or financial support can fully replace. "I will be your Father, and you will be my sons and daughters, says the Lord Almighty." – 2 Corinthians 6:18 (NLT)

The Lifelong Impact of an Engaged Father

Children thrive when they have a loving, engaged, and intentional father. Children with present fathers are more likely to excel in school. They develop higher self-esteem and confidence. They are more likely to build strong relationships and avoid destructive behaviors. "The father of godly children has cause for joy. What a pleasure to have children who are wise." – Proverbs 23:24 (NLT) Fathers play a unique and irreplaceable role in shaping their children's development. No one can replace the role of a father.

The Psychological and Emotional Effects of Father Absence

The statistics are alarming. Children without fathers face greater challenges in almost every area of life. Fatherless children are more likely to suffer from depression and anxiety. They are more prone to behavioral issues and delinquency. They have a higher risk of substance abuse and criminal activity. They struggle with trust and relationships as they grow older. According to a study by the U.S. Census Bureau, children raised in father-absent homes are: 4 times more likely to live in poverty. 7 times more likely to become pregnant as teenagers. More likely to struggle academically and drop out of school. A father's absence leaves a spiritual, emotional, and psychological wound that many children carry into adulthood. "Fathers, do not provoke your children to anger by the way you treat them. Rather, bring them up with the discipline and instruction that comes from the Lord." – Ephesians 6:4 (NLT)

Why Many Fathers Struggle with Presence

Even fathers who are in the home often struggle with being

fully present. The pressures of work and financial responsibility pull them away. Technology and social media distractions take their attention. Unresolved trauma and emotional struggles keep them distant. I know this personally. There were times when I was physically there, but mentally checked out. My children would speak to me, and instead of being engaged, I would be scrolling on my phone or thinking about work. But then I saw the look in their eyes. They needed me—fully, completely, attentively. That was my wake-up call. I had to shift my priorities and become truly present in my children's lives.

Overcoming Distraction & Absence:

1. Set specific "no-phone" time when with your children.
2. Prioritize daily quality time—reading, playing, talking.
3. Become intentional about knowing their thoughts, struggles, and dreams.

"Be present in the moment, for each day is a gift from the Lord."
– Ecclesiastes 3:12-13 (NLT)

The Spiritual Responsibility of Fathers

A father's presence is not just about providing and protecting— it is about leading spiritually. Fathers set the tone for the spiritual foundation of the home. A father's faith will often be the faith of his children. Fathers must cover their children in prayer and biblical instruction. "But as for me and my family, we will serve the Lord." – Joshua 24:15 (NLT) If we as fathers do not guide our children in the ways of the Lord, the world will guide them in the ways of destruction.

How to Be a More Present Father Today

Here are practical steps to become more engaged and present in your child's life:

1. Prioritize Quality Time:
   Eat meals together as a family—no phones, no TV.
   Create special one-on-one time with each child.
   Be involved in their hobbies, interests, and education.

"Teach us to realize the brevity of life, so that we may grow in wisdom." – Psalm 90:12 (NLT)

2. Lead with Love and Authority
   Discipline with wisdom, not anger.
   Teach through example—show what integrity, respect, and faith look like.
   Encourage and affirm your children daily.

"So encourage each other and build each other up, just as you are already doing." – 1 Thessalonians 5:11 (NLT)

3. Be Physically, Mentally, and Spiritually Present
   Put away distractions when you're with your children.
   Pray with them, study scripture together, and model a relationship with God.
   Let them see your presence as a source of safety, wisdom, and strength.

"Commit your actions to the Lord, and your plans will succeed." – Proverbs 16:3 (NLT)

Final Call to Fathers: Your Presence is Power

Your children do not need a perfect father—they need a present one. They need to feel your love. They need to hear your wisdom. They need to know that you will always be there for them. The most important thing a father can give his children is himself. "I could have no greater joy than to hear that my children are following the truth." – 3 John 1:4 (NLT)

4

Chapter 4: Breaking Generational Curses – Overcoming the Sins of Our Fathers

The Burden of Generational Sin

Many fathers today are carrying the sins, struggles, and wounds of the men who came before them. Some were raised in homes where anger was the norm. Others grew up fatherless and never learned how to be a father. Some saw patterns of addiction, abuse, or neglect repeated for generations. This is called a generational curse—a cycle of dysfunction, sin, and trauma that passes from father to son, from one generation to the next. But through Christ, these curses can be broken. "The Lord is slow to anger and filled with unfailing love, forgiving every kind of sin and rebellion. But he does not excuse the guilty. He lays the sins of the parents upon their children; the entire family is affected— even children in the third and fourth generations." – Numbers 14:18 (NLT) Generational curses are not just psychological— they are spiritual. The struggles you face today as a father may not have started with you, but they can end with you.

Recognizing the Generational Curses in Your Life

Before we can break a curse, we must identify it. Ask yourself: What negative patterns have been present in my family for generations? Were the men in your family emotionally distant or abusive? Was there a history of poverty, addiction, or divorce? Did your father fail to lead spiritually, leaving a void of faith in your family? Have the men in your family struggled with lust, infidelity, or pride? If you can recognize a pattern of struggle in your lineage, then you may be battling a generational curse. "The people answered, 'It's because our ancestors worshiped idols and did evil in the sight of the Lord, so the Lord has brought disaster upon us.'" – Jeremiah 44:22 (NLT) But here is the good news—the power of Yahshua (Jesus) is greater than any curse.

The Spiritual Authority to Break Generational Curses

Through Christ, you have been given authority to break the chains of the past. You are not bound by the failures of your father. You are not destined to repeat the mistakes of your bloodline. You are a new creation in Christ, empowered to lead your family differently. "This means that anyone who belongs to Christ has become a new person. The old life is gone; a new life has begun!" – 2 Corinthians 5:17 (NLT) If the men before you failed, you do not have to. If your father left, you can stay. If your bloodline was marked by sin, you can lead your family in righteousness. Through faith, prayer, and discipline, the cycle can be broken.

How to Break Generational Curses in Your Family

Here are the five key steps to breaking the cycle of generational sin:

1. Repent for the Sins of Your Fathers

Although the sin was not yours, you must acknowledge its presence and seek God's forgiveness on behalf of your bloodline. Confess the struggles that have plagued your family. Ask God to cleanse and redeem your family line. Commit to being the man who changes the story. "But if we confess our sins to him, he is faithful and just to forgive us our sins and to cleanse us from all wickedness." – 1 John 1:9 (NLT)

2. Declare a New Legacy Over Your Children

A curse is only effective when it is left unchallenged. Speak life over your children. Proclaim that they will be free from the struggles of past generations. Pray over them daily, covering them in God's protection and wisdom. Break every spoken word curse that may have been passed down. "Death and life are in the power of the tongue, and those who love it will eat its fruit." – Proverbs 18:21 (NLT)

3. Change Your Habits and Daily Choices

Breaking a curse is not just spiritual—it is practical. If addiction was in your family, stay away from destructive habits. If pride was your father's downfall, embrace humility and wisdom. If anger destroyed your household, choose peace and self-control. "Do not be misled: 'Bad company corrupts good character.' Come back to your senses as you ought, and stop sinning." – 1 Corinthians 15:33-34 (NLT) A new legacy begins

23

with small, daily choices.

4. Build a New Spiritual Foundation for Your Family

Many generational curses exist because of spiritual neglect. Establish a family altar—pray together daily. Read the Bible as a household. Teach your children God's ways, so they do not repeat past mistakes. "But if you refuse to serve the Lord, then choose today whom you will serve... But as for me and my family, we will serve the Lord." – Joshua 24:15 (NLT) Your children will follow your lead. Show them what it means to be a father who walks with God.

5. Surround Yourself With Righteous Men

Breaking a curse is difficult to do alone. Find godly men who will sharpen and encourage you. Be part of a strong church and men's fellowship. Be a mentor to other fathers who are breaking their own chains. "Plans fail when there is no counsel, but with many advisers they succeed." – Proverbs 15:22 (NLT) The battle is not just for you—it's for future generations.

The Generational Blessing – What Happens When You Break the Curse

When a father breaks a generational curse, the effects ripple for generations. Your children will grow up in a home filled with love, not fear. Your family will experience blessings instead of burdens. Your legacy will be one of faith, strength, and righteousness. "But the love of the Lord remains forever with those who fear him. His salvation extends to the children's children of those who are faithful to his covenant." – Psalm 103:17-18 (NLT) Your decision today will affect your children, your grandchildren, and generations to come.

Final Call to Fathers: Your Bloodline Can Be Healed

Your past does not define you. Your father's failures are not your destiny. You have been chosen to rewrite your family's history. Step into your God-given authority. Break the cycles of dysfunction and destruction. Lead your family into a new future, built on faith, wisdom, and love. "For he issued his laws to Jacob; he gave his instructions to Israel. He commanded our ancestors to teach them to their children, so the next generation might know them— even the children not yet born— and they in turn will teach their own children." – Psalm 78:5-6 (NLT)

5

Chapter 5: Fatherhood and the Power of Words – Speaking Life Over Your Children

The Power of a Father's Voice

A father's words are among the most powerful forces in a child's life. Words shape identity, confidence, and self-worth. Words can either build up or destroy. Words spoken in childhood echo into adulthood. What you say to your children—and how you say it—can influence their entire future. "The tongue can bring death or life; those who love to talk will reap the consequences." – Proverbs 18:21 (NLT) As fathers, we must choose our words carefully, intentionally, and wisely.

The Science of Words – How Words Affect the Brain and Identity

Scientific studies show that a child's brain is deeply shaped by their father's words. Positive words create strong neural pathways of confidence and self-belief. Negative words increase stress levels and self-doubt. Affirmation and encouragement improve emotional intelligence and resilience. A study from Harvard University found that children who receive consistent verbal affirmation from their parents develop: Higher self-esteem. Better problem-solving skills. Healthier emotional regulation. On the other hand, children who grow up hearing constant criticism and negativity are more likely to struggle with: Anxiety and depression. A lack of confidence and motivation. Difficulty forming healthy relationships. "Kind words are like honey— sweet to the soul and healthy for the body." – Proverbs 16:24 (NLT) A father's words carry the power to bless or curse his child's life.

The Biblical Importance of a Father's Words

The Bible teaches that a father's words have divine power. God spoke creation into existence—our words have creative power. Yahshua (Jesus) healed with His words—our words can bring healing or harm. Fathers in the Bible spoke blessings over their children, and those words determined their future. "Then Isaac said to Jacob, 'Come closer so I can touch you... May God give you the dew of heaven and the richness of the earth... May nations serve you and peoples bow down to you.'" – Genesis 27:26-29 (NLT) Just as Isaac's blessing shaped Jacob's destiny, your words will shape your child's future.

The Words Fathers Must Speak to Their Children

1. Words of Identity – Telling your child who they are
Affirm their worth and value. Tell them they are loved unconditionally. Speak life over their dreams and purpose. Say

27

This: "You are special. You are chosen by God. You have a purpose." "You are a child of God. You belong to Christ, and you are His heir." – Galatians 3:26 (NLT)

2. Words of Encouragement – Building your child's confidence

Celebrate their efforts, not just their achievements. Encourage them when they fail—help them grow. Let them know you believe in them. Say This: "I am proud of you. Keep going. You are capable of great things." "So encourage each other and build each other up, just as you are already doing." – 1 Thessalonians 5:11 (NLT)

3. Words of Protection – Covering them in wisdom and prayer

Warn them against the dangers of the world with love, not fear. Pray over them daily, asking God to guard their hearts and minds. Teach them spiritual discernment. Say This: "God is with you. No weapon formed against you will prosper." "For the Lord is your security. He will keep your foot from being caught in a trap." – Proverbs 3:26 (NLT)

4. Words of Guidance – Leading them in wisdom and faith

Teach them biblical principles for success. Model integrity and godliness through your words and actions. Give them wise counsel, showing them the right path. Say This: "Seek wisdom first. Honor God in all you do." "Seek his will in all you do, and he will show you which path to take." – Proverbs 3:6 (NLT)

5. Words of Love – Expressing warmth and affection

Tell your children you love them every single day. Hug them, hold them, and reassure them with your voice. Let them know that nothing they do can change your love for them. Say This: "I love you, and nothing will ever change that." "And may you have the power to understand, as all God's people should, how wide, how long, how high, and how deep his love is." – Ephesians 3:18 (NLT)

The Words Fathers Must Avoid

Just as words can build up, they can also destroy. Criticism can make children feel like they are never enough. Harsh words can break a child's spirit. Sarcasm and negativity can plant seeds of insecurity. The Bible warns against using words carelessly: "Don't use foul or abusive language. Let everything you say be good and helpful, so that your words will be an encouragement to those who hear them." – Ephesians 4:29 (NLT) Avoid Saying: "You'll never amount to anything." "Why can't you be like other kids?" "You always mess things up." Instead, speak words that heal and uplift.

How to Change the Way You Speak to Your Children

If you have spoken harsh words in the past, it is never too late to change. Apologize to your children if needed. Commit to speaking life over them daily. Pray and ask God to help you control your tongue. "The heart of the godly thinks carefully before speaking; the mouth of the wicked overflows with evil words." – Proverbs 15:28 (NLT) Your words have the power to change your child's future.

The Father's Daily Affirmation Over His Children

Fathers, pray this over your children every day:

29

"Lord, I bless my children today. I speak life over them. They are loved, they are chosen, they are strong, and they are called by You. May they walk in wisdom, courage, and faith. May they know their worth, and may they always seek Your truth. I declare that no weapon formed against them will prosper. In Yahshua's (Jesus') name, Amen."

Final Call to Fathers: Speak Life, Not Death

Your children are listening. What will they hear? What will they believe about themselves because of your words? What legacy will you leave with your voice? You have the power to shape their future with your words. Speak life. Every day.

Scriptures That Speak Life

You are a beloved child of God. (Romans 8:17)

You are a gift from God. (Psalm 127:3)

You are special and unique. (Isaiah 64:8)

You were created for a purpose. (Ephesians 2:10)

God has a special plan for your life. (Jeremiah 29:11)

You were lovingly and intentionally created by God. (Psalm 139:14)

You are unconditionally loved. (Romans 8:35)

You have been set apart. (I Peter 2:9)

You can hear and recognize God's voice and obey His instruction. (John 10:27)

Your steps are ordered by God. (Psalm 37:23)

God is always with you. (Deuteronomy 31:6)

You have victory in every area of your life. (I John 5:4)

6

Chapter 6: The Role of Discipline – Balancing Authority and Love

Discipline is Love, Not Control

Many fathers struggle with how to discipline their children effectively. Some fathers are too harsh, leading with anger instead of love. Others are too passive, avoiding discipline out of guilt or fear. Some were raised in homes where discipline was abusive, and they don't want to repeat that cycle. But biblical discipline is not about control—it's about correction, guidance, and love. "For the Lord disciplines those he loves, and he punishes each one he accepts as his child." – Hebrews 12:6 (NLT) Discipline is not about punishment—it is about teaching. Our goal as fathers is not to break our children's spirits, but to shape their character.

What the Bible Teaches About Discipline

The world's view of discipline is often extreme—either abusive or non-existent. But the Bible teaches a balance between discipline and love. Fathers must discipline their children, or they will suffer. Discipline must be done with wisdom, not out of frustration. The goal of discipline is to teach, not to harm. "Discipline your children while there is hope. Otherwise you will ruin their lives." – Proverbs 19:18 (NLT) If we fail to discipline our children, the world will do it for us—and much more harshly.

The Dangers of Lack of Discipline

Many fathers today avoid discipline because they fear conflict or want to be their child's friend. But the consequences of not disciplining a child are severe: They will struggle with authority and accountability in adulthood. They will lack self-control, leading to poor decision-making. They will not understand consequences, making them vulnerable to failure. "A person without self-control is like a city with broken-down walls." – Proverbs 25:28 (NLT) Lack of discipline does not create freedom—it creates destruction. A father who refuses to discipline his child is setting them up for failure.

The Dangers of Harsh or Abusive Discipline

While some fathers struggle to discipline, others discipline too harshly. Anger-driven discipline leads to resentment, not respect. Children disciplined in rage often become fearful or rebellious. Harsh discipline can break a child's spirit instead of strengthening it. The Bible warns fathers not to be too harsh: "Fathers, do not provoke your children to anger by the way you treat them. Rather, bring them up with the discipline and instruction that comes from the Lord." – Ephesians 6:4 (NLT) Correction should be firm but fair. Discipline should be consistent but never cruel. A father must guide with love, not intimidation. If we discipline out of frustration, we are not leading—we are reacting.

The Balance: How to Discipline with Authority and Love

1. Discipline Must Be Clear and Consistent

Children need to know the rules and expectations. Discipline should be applied fairly, not based on emotions. Be consistent— do not enforce rules one day and ignore them the next. "People who accept discipline are on the pathway to life, but those who ignore correction will go astray." – Proverbs 10:17 (NLT)

2. Discipline Must Be Done With Self-Control

Never discipline in the heat of anger—wait until you are calm. If you are too emotional, step away and pray before correcting. Always explain the reason for discipline to your child. "Better to be patient than powerful; better to have self-control than to conquer a city." – Proverbs 16:32 (NLT)

3. Use Different Forms of Discipline Based on the Situation

Discipline is not one-size-fits-all. Different situations require different approaches: Natural Consequences: Let them experience the result of their actions. Loss of Privileges: Remove something meaningful as a consequence. Correction Through Conversation: Teach through wisdom, not just punishment. Physical Discipline (When Appropriate): The Bible does not forbid spanking, but it must be done with control, wisdom, and love—never in anger. "Those who spare the rod of discipline hate their children. Those who love their children care enough to discipline them." – Proverbs 13:24 (NLT)

4. Discipline Must Always Be Followed by Love and Affirmation

Correct your child, then remind them of your love. After discipline, speak words of encouragement and identity. Make sure they know the correction was for their good, not out of anger. "The Lord is compassionate and merciful, slow to get angry and filled with unfailing love." – Psalm 103:8 (NLT)

Say This After Discipline:

"I love you, and I correct you because I want you to grow." "I am proud of you, and I know you can do better." "This discipline is not punishment—it's preparation for life." Children must always know that discipline is love in action.

The Power of a Father's Discipline

When a father disciplines with wisdom, love, and consistency: His children will grow up with self-discipline and respect. They will learn to make wise choices. They will trust and respect their father, not resent him. "Correct your children, and they will give you peace of mind; they will make your heart glad." – Proverbs 29:17 (NLT) Discipline is not about control—it is about preparation. A father's discipline is what prepares his children for life.

Final Call to Fathers: Lead with Strength and Love

Be firm, but never cruel. Be consistent, but never irrational. Be loving, but never weak. Your children need your discipline to grow into strong men and women. Be the father who corrects with wisdom and leads with love. "My children, listen when your father corrects you. Pay attention and learn good judgment, for I am giving you good guidance. Don't turn away from my instructions." – Proverbs 4:1-2 (NLT)

7

Chapter 7: Teaching Responsibility and Work Ethic – Raising Hardworking, Accountable Children

Responsibility Starts at Home

A father's role is not just to provide—it is to prepare. A responsible child grows into a responsible adult. A child with strong work ethic will be prepared for success. A child who is held accountable will develop discipline and integrity. But responsibility and work ethic are not automatic. Fathers must teach them. "A wise child brings joy to a father; a foolish child brings grief to a mother." – Proverbs 10:1 (NLT) If we fail to instill responsibility in our children, they will struggle when life requires it.

Why Responsibility & Work Ethic Matter

A lack of responsibility and work ethic creates weak men and women. Entitlement grows when responsibility is not taught.

Laziness develops when work ethic is not required. Excuses replace action when accountability is absent. The world does not reward laziness—it punishes it. If we do not teach our children to work hard, take responsibility, and be accountable, they will struggle in every area of life. "Lazy people want much but get little, but those who work hard will prosper." – Proverbs 13:4 (NLT)

Breaking My Own Cycle of Over-Providing and Under-Teaching

I grew up in a military household, where discipline and hard work were non-negotiable. My father was strict but fair, and he expected me to take responsibility for my actions and my future. But when I became a father, I found myself overcompensating. I wanted to make life easier for my kids than it was for me. I wanted them to have every opportunity, without the struggle. I wanted them to be comfortable, rather than challenged. That was a mistake. Comfort breeds complacency, and complacency leads to weakness. "Endure hardship as discipline; God is treating you as his children. For what children are not disciplined by their father?" – Hebrews 12:7 (NLT) That was my wake-up call. I had to teach my children the way my father taught me— through action, responsibility, and work.

How My Children Changed Once I Became Intentional

They started taking initiative instead of waiting to be told. They became more disciplined in their daily routines. They developed a deeper appreciation for the things they had. Most importantly, they stopped expecting things to be handed to them and started working for what they wanted. That is how generational cycles are changed.

Encouragement to Fathers Who Struggle With This

If you are a father who has been over-providing but under-teaching, I want to encourage you: It's not too late to change. You don't have to take everything away—you just have to shift your approach. Your children will respect you more for teaching them discipline than for giving them handouts. "Commit your actions to the Lord, and your plans will succeed." – Proverbs 16:3 (NLT) Our job as fathers is not to give our children an easy life. Our job is to prepare them for life.

How to Teach Responsibility to Your Children

Responsibility is not given—it is taught. Work ethic is not automatic—it is built through experience. Accountability is not optional—it is necessary for growth. Here's how fathers can raise responsible children:

1. Start Early – Give Them Responsibilities as Kids

Age-appropriate chores teach work ethic and discipline. Small responsibilities build confidence and accountability. Teach them that effort leads to reward. I have given each of my children responsibilities in the home. They know that being part of this family means contributing to the household. Example: My son is responsible for making sure the trash is taken out on time. If he forgets, he must own the consequences. "If you are faithful in little things, you will be faithful in large ones." – Luke 16:10 (NLT)

39

2. Teach the Value of Hard Work – Don't Reward Laziness

Do not give them everything for free—teach them to earn. Let them feel the satisfaction of working for what they want. Show them that nothing great in life comes without effort. I have taken my children with me to work so they could see firsthand the effort it takes to build something. I want them to understand that everything we have came from faith, discipline, and action. Example: When one of my children asked for a new toy, I encouraged them to save up for it rather than just buying it outright. "Work hard and become a leader; be lazy and become a slave." – Proverbs 12:24 (NLT)

3. Hold Them Accountable – No Excuses, No Blame

Teach them to own their mistakes instead of making excuses. Show them that actions have consequences. Do not rescue them from their failures—help them learn from them. I once watched one of my children struggle with responsibility for their schoolwork. Instead of fixing the problem for them, I let them experience the natural consequences of forgetting their assignment. After that, they never forgot again. Example: My daughter forgot to bring her school project home one day, and instead of rushing to fix it for her, I let her experience the natural consequence of not being prepared. The next time, she was more responsible. "Don't be misled—you cannot mock the justice of God. You will always harvest what you plant." – Galatians 6:7 (NLT)

4. Set the Example – Work Hard and Take Responsibility Yourself

Children learn more from watching than listening. Model discipline, responsibility, and work ethic. Let them see you work hard, own your mistakes, and be accountable. I wake up early every morning to handle my responsibilities before my children wake up, so that when they see me, they see a father who is fully engaged in life. Example: "Son, I got home late because I had to finish my work properly. A man does his job well." "Do your work willingly, as though you were serving the Lord himself." – Colossians 3:23 (NLT)

Raising Sons & Daughters Who Are Not Afraid of Hard Work

Make work part of life, not a punishment. Celebrate their effort, not just results. Help them find joy in discipline and progress. "Take pride in your work, for when you do, it brings honor to God." – Proverbs 22:29 (NLT) Children who grow up learning responsibility and work ethic will be strong, independent, and successful.

The Father's Daily Affirmation Over His Children

Fathers, pray this over your children every day:
"Lord, I pray my children will be hardworking, responsible, and disciplined. May they grow in wisdom, strength, and integrity. Let them take ownership of their actions and never fear hard work. May they be faithful in little, so they can be trusted with much. May they always glorify You in all that they do. In Yahshua's (Jesus') name, Amen."

Final Call to Fathers: Prepare Your Children for Life

Teach them responsibility early. Instill work ethic through experience. Hold them accountable with love. The greatest gift you can give your children is the ability to stand on their own.

"Start children off on the way they should go, and even when they are old, they will not turn from it." – Proverbs 22:6 (NLT)

8

Chapter 8: Financial Provision – Breaking the Cycle of Scarcity and Embracing Abundance

A Father's Role as a Financial Provider

Many fathers believe financial provision means just bringing home a paycheck. But true provision goes beyond just meeting material needs—it means: Teaching financial responsibility to your children. Breaking generational cycles of poverty and scarcity. Positioning your family for long-term abundance. Instilling a mindset of stewardship, not just consumption. I once thought that as long as I was making money, I was fulfilling my role. But I realized that wealth without wisdom is temporary. Fathers must not only provide financially but also equip their families with the mindset and knowledge to sustain abundance. "A good man leaves an inheritance to his children's children, but the sinner's wealth passes to the godly." – Proverbs 13:22 (NLT) Abundance is not about chasing money—it is about aligning with God's principles of provision.

Breaking the Scarcity Mindset

I grew up watching people work hard just to get by. The constant struggle to pay bills. Living paycheck to paycheck. Fear of losing what little was gained. This scarcity mindset was deeply ingrained, and for years, I carried it into my own life. I worked tirelessly but was always stressed about finances. I thought financial stability meant more hours, more jobs, more hustle. I saw money as something hard to get and easy to lose. But God never intended for His children to live in fear and lack. "And my God will supply all your needs from his glorious riches, which have been given to us in Christ Yahshua (Jesus)." – Philippians 4:19 (NLT)

Shifting to a Mindset of Abundance

The day I truly surrendered my finances to God, I had a revelation: Abundance is our birthright, but it must be stewarded well. Financial provision isn't about working harder—it's about working smarter. God honors faith-driven action, not fear-driven labor. Once I aligned my financial life with biblical principles, everything changed. I stopped chasing money and started attracting opportunities. I became intentional about financial education for my children. I put systems in place to ensure long-term wealth for my family. "Seek the Kingdom of God above all else, and live righteously, and he will give you everything you need." – Matthew 6:33 (NLT)

The 4 Pillars of Financial Provision

1. Tithing and Giving – Honoring God With Your Finances
2. Stewardship – Managing Money With Wisdom
3. Generational Wealth – Creating Lasting Financial Security
4. Teaching Financial Literacy – Equipping the Next Generation

1. Tithing and Giving – Honoring God With Your Finances

God must be FIRST in your financial life. Tithing is an act of obedience, trust, and partnership with God. Giving breaks the chains of greed and scarcity. I used to hold on tightly to every dollar because I feared lack. But once I committed to tithing consistently, my financial situation shifted. Unexpected opportunities opened up. Doors I never imagined began to unlock. I was no longer living in constant worry about money. "Bring all the tithes into the storehouse so there will be enough food in my Temple. If you do," says the Lord of Heaven's Armies, "I will open the windows of heaven for you. I will pour out a blessing so great you won't have enough room to take it in! Try it! Put me to the test!" – Malachi 3:10 (NLT)

2. Stewardship – Managing Money With Wisdom

Many people pray for financial breakthroughs but lack the discipline to manage what they already have. Budgeting is a tool, not a burden. Debt should be minimized, not embraced. Impulse spending is the enemy of financial growth. I learned to tell my money where to go instead of wondering where it went. I created a budget that prioritized needs, investments, and savings. I cut unnecessary expenses that weren't adding value to my life. I focused on being a wise steward instead of an emotional spender. "The wise have wealth and luxury, but fools spend whatever they get." – Proverbs 21:20 (NLT)

3. Generational Wealth – Creating Lasting Financial Security

Wealth is not about how much you make—it's about how much you keep and grow. Financial independence allows fathers to focus on their families. Generational wealth ensures your children don't start from zero. Real wealth is built through assets, not just income. I have taken intentional steps to build generational wealth for my children. Investing in assets that appreciate over time. Educating my children on financial literacy. Setting up trust funds and long-term investment strategies. "The rich rule over the poor, and the borrower is servant to the lender." – Proverbs 22:7 (NLT)

4. Teaching Financial Literacy – Equipping the Next Generation

Financial education should start in childhood. Children must learn how to manage money before they earn money. If we don't teach them, the world will. I actively teach my children: How to budget and save. The importance of investing early. How to avoid debt and live within their means. "Train up a child in the way he should go, and when he is old he will not depart from it." – Proverbs 22:6 (NLT) Our schools do not teach financial wisdom—so it is our responsibility as fathers.

Encouragement for Fathers Struggling With Financial Provision

I have felt the stress of financial hardship. The pressure to provide. The fear of not having enough. The frustration of seeing hard work not always pay off. But here is what I've learned: God is faithful to those who trust Him. Financial breakthroughs come when faith meets discipline. Scarcity is a mindset that must be broken. "Commit your actions to the Lord, and your plans will succeed." – Proverbs 16:3 (NLT) If you are struggling: Surrender your finances to God. Take action—educate yourself, make a plan, and execute it. Teach your children so they do not repeat the cycle.

The Father's Daily Prayer for Financial Provision

"Lord, I thank You for being my Provider. I trust that You will supply all my needs according to Your riches and glory. Help me to be a wise steward of my finances, to give generously, and to teach my children financial wisdom. Break every spirit of lack and scarcity in my life. Lead me to opportunities that align with Your will. Let my family walk in abundance and never in fear. In Yahshua's (Jesus') name, Amen."

Final Call to Fathers: Step Into Your Financial Role

Be a provider, but also a financial teacher. Break generational curses of debt and scarcity. Align your finances with God's principles, and abundance will follow. "The blessing of the Lord makes a person rich, and he adds no sorrow with it." – Proverbs 10:22 (NLT) Your family's financial future is in your hands.

9

Chapter 9: Rebuilding Fatherhood in Communities – Restoring the Pillars of Strength

The Crisis of Fatherhood in Communities

Fatherhood is not just about raising children—it is about building strong families, strong communities, and a strong society. Yet, we are witnessing a massive crisis in fatherhood today: Fatherlessness is at an all-time high. Men are absent—not just from homes, but from communities. Young boys are growing up without male role models. Entire generations are suffering from the breakdown of families. I have seen this firsthand in my own community. The struggles of single mothers trying to raise children alone. Young men turning to crime, gangs, and violence in the absence of fathers. Daughters searching for validation in all the wrong places. The absence of strong fathers has left a void—one that is being filled by the wrong influences. "The godly walk with integrity; blessed are their children who follow them." – Proverbs 20:7 (NLT) We, as men, must rise up and take responsibility for the communities we live in.

The Impact of Fatherlessness on Communities

1. The Breakdown of the Family Structure

Fatherless homes are more vulnerable to financial hardship. Single mothers are forced to play multiple roles, often without support. Children lack discipline, structure, and emotional security. A community without strong fathers is like a house with no foundation. "A house divided against itself will not stand." – Mark 3:25 (NLT) When fathers are absent, the entire family structure weakens—leading to cycles of:

1. Poverty
2. Crime
3. Emotional instability
4. Generational fatherlessness

2. The Rise of Crime and Gang Culture

Boys without fathers seek male role models elsewhere. Without guidance, many turn to gangs, crime, and violence. Prisons are filled with men who grew up without strong fathers. Statistics show that 70% of incarcerated men grew up in fatherless homes. A missing father leads to missing discipline. A missing father leads to missing identity. A missing father leads to missing purpose. "Discipline your children, and they will give you peace of mind and will make your heart glad." – Proverbs 29:17 (NLT) Fathers must stand in the gap before the streets claim their sons.

3. The Emotional and Psychological Toll on Children

Boys without fathers struggle with identity and self-worth. Girls without fathers are more likely to suffer from insecurity and toxic relationships. Children with absentee fathers are at a greater risk of depression, substance abuse, and mental illness. "Fathers, do not provoke your children to anger by the way you treat them. Rather, bring them up with the discipline and instruction that comes from the Lord." – Ephesians 6:4 (NLT) A father's love, discipline, and presence create emotional security, confidence, and stability in a child's life.

Rebuilding Fatherhood in Our Communities

We cannot just talk about the problem—we must be the solution. Here's how we can rebuild fatherhood and restore communities:

1. Strengthening Fathers Through Brotherhood and Mentorship

Fathers need community, accountability, and guidance. Strong men must teach young men how to be fathers. Churches, businesses, and community centers must step up to build fatherhood initiatives. I personally make it a priority to mentor young men—especially those who lack fathers. I teach them responsibility. I help them develop a vision for their lives. I hold them accountable for their actions. "Repeat them again and again to your children. Talk about them when you are at home and when you are on the road, when you are going to bed and when you are getting up." – Deuteronomy 6:7 (NLT) Men must come together to sharpen one another and build the next generation.

2. Coaches, Teachers, and Leaders – All Men Have an Obligation

Fathers are not the only men responsible for shaping children. Coaches are father figures on the field. Teachers influence and guide children in the classroom. Pastors and mentors help build character and wisdom. "Commit your actions to the Lord, and your plans will succeed." – Proverbs 16:3 (NLT) Every man in a leadership role has the power to uplift or break down the children around them. Speak life into young men who need guidance. Encourage, correct, and challenge boys to be great. Stand in the gap for children who lack fathers. The rebuilding of fatherhood starts with every man stepping up where he is.

3. Teaching Financial Literacy and Economic Empowerment

Fathers must teach their children how to break the poverty cycle. Communities need economic education, not just survival tactics. Strong financial foundations create stability and growth. I have made it a mission to teach financial literacy in my home and community. Wealth is not about how much you make, but how much you manage wisely. Generational wealth starts with knowledge and discipline. Empowered fathers create empowered families. "Lazy people want much but get little, but those who work hard will prosper." – Proverbs 13:4 (NLT) If we want strong communities, we must create financially responsible fathers.

4. Restoring Marriage and Family Values

Children thrive when raised by both a father and a mother. Marriage creates a stable environment for children to grow. Fathers must lead in restoring the sanctity of marriage. "But 'God made them male and female' from the beginning of creation. 'This explains why a man leaves his father and mother and is joined to his wife, and the two are united into one.'" – Mark 10:6-8 (NLT) Rebuilding communities starts with rebuilding strong marriages and strong families.

The Father's Call to Action: Rebuild the Village

Be present, not just in your home, but in your community. Mentor young men who lack father figures. Create spaces for boys to grow into men. Teach financial, emotional, and spiritual discipline. Commit to strengthening marriages and families. "Blessed is the nation whose God is the Lord, the people he chose as his inheritance." – Psalm 33:12 (NLT) A nation cannot be strong if its families are weak. A family cannot be strong if its fathers are absent.

The Father's Daily Prayer for Rebuilding Communities

"Lord, I lift up the fathers in every community. Strengthen them, guide them, and give them the courage to rise up and take their place as leaders. Let us be the example our children need. Help us restore marriages, mentor the next generation, and build a legacy of righteousness. Father, use me as a vessel to heal, teach, and lead. May I be an instrument of Your will, bringing transformation to my home and my community. In Yahshua's (Jesus') name, Amen."

Final Call to Fathers: Be the Change Your Community Needs

Your leadership is needed. Your wisdom is needed. Your presence is needed. "The righteous man walks in his integrity; his children are blessed after him." – Proverbs 20:7 (NLT) Fathers, let's rebuild our homes, our families, and our communities—together.

10

Chapter 10: How Society Can Rebuild the Role of Fathers

A Call to Restore Fatherhood

The crisis of fatherhood is not just a personal issue—it is a societal issue. Broken families lead to broken communities. Broken communities lead to broken nations. The collapse of fatherhood is one of the greatest crises of our time. For too long, society has devalued the role of fathers. The media often portrays fathers as unnecessary or incompetent. Courts often strip fathers of their rights in custody battles. Workplaces demand so much from men that they are forced to neglect their families. The truth is, when fathers thrive, families thrive, and when families thrive, nations thrive. "The godly walk with integrity; blessed are their children who follow them." – Proverbs 20:7 (NLT) If we truly care about the future, we must rebuild the role of fathers in society.

The Systemic Attacks on Fatherhood

1. The Legal System and Family Courts

Many fathers are unfairly treated in custody battles. Family courts often favor mothers, even when fathers are fit parents. Fathers are often reduced to "weekend dads" or forced out of their children's lives. I have seen countless good fathers fight just to be present in their children's lives. Men who want to be active, loving fathers are often met with obstacles. Some give up, not because they don't care, but because the system has broken them. "A father to the fatherless, defender of widows—this is God, whose dwelling is holy." – Psalm 68:5 (NLT)

2. The Media's Portrayal of Fathers

TV shows and movies often depict fathers as clueless, weak, or absent. Music and entertainment push hyper-masculinity without fatherly wisdom. Men are either seen as unnecessary or as financial providers, not emotional leaders. I have personally witnessed how young men are absorbing these false narratives. They don't see real fatherhood modeled in society. They don't aspire to be great fathers because they don't see it valued. Many grow up believing that being a father is a burden, not a blessing. "The father of godly children has cause for joy. What a pleasure to have children who are wise." – Proverbs 23:24 (NLT)

3. Work and Economic Pressures

Fathers are expected to work long hours just to provide. Many jobs demand so much that family time is sacrificed. Men often feel torn between providing financially and being present at home. I personally struggled with this balance. I thought being a great father meant working harder and making more money. But my children needed my presence more than they needed more "stuff." "Don't wear yourself out trying to get rich. Be wise enough to know when to quit." – Proverbs 23:4 (NLT) If society truly wants strong families, it must support fathers in being present.

How Society Can Restore Fatherhood

The solution is not just personal—it must be cultural, legal, and systemic. Here's how we can rebuild the role of fathers in society:

1. Reforming Family Laws to Support Fathers

Fathers should have equal parental rights in custody cases. There must be more support for men seeking active fatherhood roles. Courts should prioritize the child's right to have a loving father. I have seen too many good men being stripped of their ability to be active fathers. We must fight for fair policies that recognize the importance of fathers. Every child deserves both parents when possible. "Blessed are those who act justly, who always do what is right." – Psalm 106:3 (NLT)

2. Changing the Narrative About Fathers in Media

Hollywood and entertainment must stop portraying fathers as weak or unnecessary. We need more books, movies, and shows that uplift and honor fatherhood. Men must be intentional about telling their own stories and showing strong fatherhood. I have seen how media shapes minds. When fathers are glorified, young men aspire to be great fathers. When fatherhood is devalued, young men abandon their role. "Finally, brothers and sisters, whatever is true, whatever is noble, whatever is right, whatever is pure, whatever is lovely, whatever is admirable— if anything is excellent or praiseworthy—think about such things." – Philippians 4:8 (NLT)

3. Encouraging Work-Life Balance for Fathers

Employers must recognize that fathers need time with their children. Workplaces should offer paternity leave and flexible schedules. Fathers should not have to choose between career success and family success. I personally had to restructure my life to prioritize my family. I realized that no amount of money could replace lost time with my children. True success is having a thriving family, not just a thriving bank account. "Better to have little, with fear for the Lord, than to have great treasure and inner turmoil." – Proverbs 15:16 (NLT) Fathers must demand change in the workplace so they can be fully present at home.

4. Strengthening Fatherhood Education and Mentorship

Young men must be taught how to be fathers before they become fathers. Fatherhood programs should be implemented in schools and churches. Men must mentor the next generation, passing down wisdom. I have personally seen how mentorship changes lives. When young men have father figures, they thrive. When they lack guidance, they seek validation in the wrong places. "Where there is no guidance, a people falls, but in an abundance of counselors there is safety." – Proverbs 11:14 (NLT) We must invest in fatherhood education so that young men are equipped for the role.

The Father's Call to Action: Be the Change

Fight for policies that support fathers. Reject negative portray-als of fathers in media. Demand workplaces that respect family values. Mentor young men and teach them about fatherhood. "Let us not grow weary of doing good, for in due season we will reap, if we do not give up." – Galatians 6:9 (NLT) The world needs fathers. Families need fathers. Our future depends on fathers.

The Father's Daily Prayer for Society to Restore Fatherhood

"Lord, I pray for the restoration of fatherhood in our commu-nities and our world. Let society recognize the value of fathers. Let the laws be fair, workplaces be balanced, and media reflect the truth about fatherhood. Let men rise up to take their place as leaders, protectors, and providers. May we stand together, fight for our families, and build a legacy of strong, godly fathers. In Yahshua's (Jesus') name, Amen."

Final Call to Society: Rebuild Fatherhood, Rebuild the Future

A society that strengthens fathers will strengthen families. A society that weakens fathers will suffer the consequences. It's time for the world to acknowledge, honor, and uplift fathers once again. "His preaching will turn the hearts of fathers to their children, and the hearts of children to their fathers. Otherwise I will come and strike the land with a curse."- Malachi 4:6 (NLT) Fathers, the world needs you. Society, it's time to rebuild.

11

Chapter 11: The Ultimate Fatherhood Blueprint

A Fatherhood Blueprint for the Ages

Fatherhood is not something we stumble into—it is a calling, a mission, and a divine responsibility. Yet, many fathers do not have a clear blueprint for success. Some had no fathers to teach them. Some are learning through trial and error. Some feel lost, overwhelmed, and unsure of their role. But God never leaves us without direction. He has laid out a divine blueprint for fatherhood—a path to lead, protect, and nurture our children with wisdom, love, and strength. "Your word is a lamp to guide my feet and a light for my path." – Psalm 119:105 (NLT) This chapter lays out the ultimate fatherhood blueprint—one that any man can follow to become a father of impact, integrity, and divine purpose.

The 5 Pillars of the Ultimate Fatherhood Blueprint

1. Spiritual Leadership – A Father's Divine Responsibility

A father must lead his home in faith. He must pray over his children, teach them the Word, and model godly character. He is not just a provider—he is the priest of his household. I have learned that when I align myself with God, my children align with me. If I am spiritually disconnected, my home is spiritually unprotected. "As for me and my family, we will serve the Lord." – Joshua 24:15 (NLT)

2. Emotional Presence – Giving Your Children More Than Just Time

Children need more than a father who is physically present. They need a father who listens, encourages, and engages. A father's love and affirmation shape a child's confidence. I have seen my children light up when I truly listen to them. They feel seen, heard, and valued when I give them my full attention. "Fathers, do not provoke your children to anger by the way you treat them. Rather, bring them up with the discipline and instruction that comes from the Lord." – Ephesians 6:4 (NLT)

3. Discipline and Wisdom – Teaching Accountability and Strength

A father must guide his children with wisdom and correction. Discipline is not about control—it is about shaping character. Correction must be done in love, not in anger. I have learned that discipline, when done right, builds trust rather than fear. My children know I correct them because I love them, not because I want power over them. "My child, don't reject the Lord's discipline, and don't be upset when he corrects you. For the Lord corrects those he loves, just as a father corrects a child in whom he delights." – Proverbs 3:11-12 (NLT)

4. *Financial Stewardship – Providing and Teaching Wealth Wisdom*

A father must provide for his family—not just financially, but with wisdom. He must teach his children financial responsibility and stewardship. Generational wealth is not just money—it is mindset, discipline, and vision. I have seen the impact of teaching my children how to manage, save, and invest. Their understanding of money will determine their future success. "Good planning and hard work lead to prosperity, but hasty shortcuts lead to poverty." – Proverbs 21:5 (NLT)

5. *Legacy and Leadership – Raising Kings and Queens*

A father's ultimate role is to leave a legacy of righteousness. His children should be better, stronger, and wiser because of his leadership. A great father does not just raise children—he raises future leaders. I have realized that every lesson I teach my children now will impact generations after me. The time, love, and wisdom I pour into them today will ripple into eternity. "A good man leaves an inheritance to his children's children." – Proverbs 13:22 (NLT)

The Father's Daily Blueprint for Success

Every day, a father must commit to 5 non-negotiables to ensure he follows the ultimate fatherhood blueprint:

1. Morning Prayer & Scripture Reading – Start the day by covering your family in prayer.
2. Affirm Your Children – Speak words of life over them before they go into the world.

3. Teach & Guide – Take every moment as an opportunity to teach and guide them.

4. Lead by Example – Live the lessons you want them to learn.

5. End the Day with Gratitude & Reflection – Thank God for the gift of fatherhood and reflect on ways to improve.

"Be strong and courageous. Do not be afraid or discouraged. For the Lord your God is with you wherever you go." – Joshua 1:9 (NLT)

Encouragement for Fathers: No One is Perfect, But Every Father Can Improve

You don't have to be perfect—you just have to be present. You don't have to have all the answers—you just have to be willing to grow. Your past mistakes don't define you—your commitment to change does. I have made mistakes as a father, but I have also learned from them. The greatest fathers are those who continue to grow, learn, and lead. Your children don't need a perfect dad—they need a present and intentional one. "The righteous keep moving forward, and those with clean hands become stronger and stronger." – Job 17:9 (NLT)

The Father's Daily Prayer for Strength and Wisdom

"Lord, I thank You for the gift of fatherhood. Guide me in wisdom, patience, and love. Strengthen me to be the leader my family needs. Teach me to raise my children with faith, integrity, and purpose. Let my actions align with Your will. Help me to leave a legacy of righteousness that will impact generations. In Yahshua's (Jesus') name, Amen."

Final Call to Fathers: Embrace the Blueprint, Change the World

You were chosen for this role. Your leadership will impact generations. Your presence is a divine assignment. "Commit everything you do to the Lord. Trust him, and he will help you." – Psalm 37:5 (NLT) Fathers, it is time to step into the role God created for you. This blueprint is not just a guide—it is a mission. Your family, your community, and the world need you.

12

Chapter 12: The 30-Day Fatherhood Challenge – Becoming the Father You Were Called to Be

The Power of Intentional Fatherhood

Becoming a great father does not happen by accident. It requires: Intentionality – Choosing to be fully present each day. Growth – Seeking wisdom and improving daily. Discipline – Practicing what you preach. For many fathers, the greatest challenge is consistency. We start strong but lose momentum. We have good intentions but get distracted. We love our children but don't always show it the way they need. That's why this 30-day challenge is designed to: Help you build daily habits of intentional fatherhood. Strengthen your bond with your children. Challenge you to lead with wisdom, love, and faith. "Whatever you do, work at it with all your heart, as working for the Lord, not for human masters." – Colossians 3:23 (NLT) Let's commit to 30 days of intentional fatherhood—because your children deserve the best version of you.

How This Challenge Works

Each day, you will focus on a specific action that strengthens your fatherhood journey. Some days will challenge your mindset. Some will push you to take action. All will help you grow as a father. At the end of 30 days, you will have: Built stronger relationships with your children. Developed habits that will last a lifetime. Become a more confident and intentional father. "Teach us to realize the brevity of life, so that we may grow in wisdom." – Psalm 90:12 (NLT)

The 30-Day Fatherhood Challenge

Week 1: Laying the Foundation

Day 1: Pray for Your Children – Start your day by praying over their lives, futures, and hearts.

Day 2: Have an Eye-Level Conversation – Get down to your child's level and truly listen.

Day 3: Speak Life – Affirm your children with words of encouragement.

Day 4: Be Fully Present – Turn off distractions and spend quality time together.

Day 5: Create a One-on-One Ritual – Establish a habit of spending individual time with each child.

Day 6: Read Scripture Together – Teach your children the Word of God in a simple and engaging way.

Day 7: Lead with Love and Discipline – Correct your child with patience and wisdom.

Week 2: Strengthening Emotional Bonds

Day 8: Tell Your Child You Are Proud of Them – Even if they

know, they need to hear it.

Day 9: Ask Deeper Questions – Go beyond "How was your day?" and learn about their dreams.

Day 10: Apologize for Any Past Mistakes – Show them humility and accountability.

Day 11: Make Them Laugh – Share joy, humor, and light-hearted moments.

Day 12: Write a Letter to Your Child – Share your love, wisdom, and prayers for them.

Day 13: Set a Family Tradition – Create something meaningful your children will remember forever.

Day 14: Teach a Life Skill – Show them something practical that will benefit them in adulthood.

Week 3: Becoming a Leader and Protector

Day 15: Create a Family Vision Statement – Define your family's values and goals.

Day 16: Share a Personal Testimony – Teach them a lesson from your own struggles and victories.

Day 17: Teach Them About Money – Show them how to save, give, and manage finances wisely.

Day 18: Take Them on a One-on-One Adventure – Do something new and memorable together.

Day 19: Model Respect for Women – Show them how to treat their mother and other women with honor.

Day 20: Teach Them About Strength and Kindness – Balance toughness with tenderness.

Day 21: Prepare Them for Real-World Challenges – Have deep conversations about peer pressure, faith, and resilience.

Week 4: Leaving a Legacy

Day 22: Help Them Set Goals – Teach them to think ahead and take action.

Day 23: Serve Together – Show them the joy of giving and helping others.

Day 24: Celebrate Their Unique Talents – Encourage them in their God-given gifts.

Day 25: Teach Them About Integrity – Explain why doing what's right matters, even when no one is watching.

Day 26: Pray Together as a Family – Establish the habit of seeking God's guidance as a unit.

Day 27: Give a Final Blessing – Speak a prophetic word of encouragement over their future.

Day 28: Reflect on the Journey – Ask your children what they've learned and how they feel about the experience.

Day 29: Commit to Lifelong Fatherhood Growth – Make a plan to continue growing as a father.

Day 30: Celebrate Together – Enjoy a special moment together and thank God for the journey.

Reflection: What This Challenge Will Do for You and Your Children

Your children will feel more loved, heard, and supported. You will grow in patience, wisdom, and leadership. Your home will be stronger, more connected, and more joyful. Most importantly, you will see God's presence move through your role as a father. "Let all that you do be done in love." – 1 Corinthians 16:14 (NLT)

The Father's Daily Prayer for Strength During the Challenge

"Lord, I commit to becoming the father You have called me to be. Strengthen me, guide me, and correct me where needed.

Help me to lead my children in love, wisdom, and faith. Give me patience when I am weary, strength when I am weak, and clarity when I feel lost. Let my children see You through me, and let our home be filled with Your presence. In Yahshua's (Jesus') name, Amen."

Final Call to Fathers: Take the Challenge, Transform Your Family

30 days of intentional fatherhood will change your life. Your children need you now more than ever. You have the power to shape their future with your love and leadership. "For I can do everything through Christ,[a] who gives me strength." – Philippians 4:13 (NLT) Fathers, take this challenge and see how God moves in your home.

13

Chapter 13: A Father's Call to Rise Up

The Defining Moment of a Father's Life

Every father faces a defining moment—a moment where he must decide who he will be. Will he be passive or present? Will he lead or follow? Will he rise or retreat? For me, that moment came when I realized my children weren't just watching me— they were becoming me. The way I spoke became the way they spoke. The way I reacted became the way they reacted. The way I lived became the way they would live. That realization hit me like a flood. I could not expect them to rise if I was unwilling to rise myself. I had to be the example of strength, wisdom, and faith that they needed. "Be on guard. Stand firm in the faith. Be courageous. Be strong." – 1 Corinthians 16:13 (NLT)

The Battle for Fatherhood – The Fight of a Lifetime

Let's be real—fatherhood is warfare. The enemy wants to keep fathers distracted, discouraged, and disengaged. Society wants to devalue fatherhood. The system wants fathers to be absent, silent, and powerless. But here's the truth: Fathers are the backbone of the home. Fathers are the protectors of the next generation. Fathers are the leaders that God has ordained. "The Lord himself will fight for you. Just stay calm." – Exodus 14:14 (NLT) We are not just fighting for ourselves. We are fighting for our sons, so they don't grow up lost. We are fighting for our daughters, so they know their worth. We are fighting for our families, so they can experience love, strength, and security.

The Turning Point – My Personal Moment of Transformation

For years, I thought being a father was just about providing. I worked hard. I brought home the paycheck. I thought that was enough. But my children needed more. They needed my presence, not just my provision. They needed my guidance, not just my discipline. They needed my love, not just my authority. I will never forget the moment I sat my children down, looked them in the eyes, and apologized for the times I wasn't fully present. I told them I was sorry for the moments I let my phone distract me. I was sorry for the moments I didn't listen to them when they needed me. I was sorry for not always being the father they deserved. Tears filled my eyes as I asked for their forgiveness—and they gave it freely. That was the day I made a covenant with God to be fully present, fully engaged, and fully committed to leading my family in faith, wisdom, and love. "A righteous person falls seven times and gets back up, but the wicked will stumble into ruin." – Proverbs 24:16 (NLT)

The Father's Pledge: A Commitment to Rise

This is your defining moment. Will you step up and lead? Will you become the father your children need? Will you rise up and take your place?

If your answer is yes, then take this pledge:

"I, [Your Name], commit to being the father God has called me to be. I will not shrink back. I will not let distractions, fear, or failure hold me back. I will be a provider, protector, and leader in my home. I will cover my children in prayer. I will teach them wisdom and truth. I will love their mother with honor and respect. I will be fully present in their lives. And I will pass down a legacy of faith, strength, and love. This is my commitment before God, my family, and myself. I will rise. In Yahshua's (Jesus') name, Amen."

Final Words: This Is Your Time

You don't have to be perfect—just present. You don't have to have all the answers—just a willing heart. You don't have to do it alone—God is with you. Fatherhood is the greatest calling on Earth. It is time to rise up and walk in it. "For God has not given us a spirit of fear and timidity, but of power, love, and self-discipline." – 2 Timothy 1:7 (NLT) Fathers, this is your moment. Take your place. Lead with faith. And never look back.

14

Chapter 14: The Future of Fatherhood – A Vision for the Next Generation

The World We Will Leave Behind

Fathers, the choices we make today will shape the world of tomorrow. The way we lead will determine the kind of men our sons become. The way we love will set the standard for how our daughters will be treated. The way we protect, teach, and guide will impact generations long after we are gone. The future of fatherhood is not just about us—it is about the legacy we leave behind. We stand at a crossroads. Will we be the generation that restores fatherhood? Will we be the men who break generational curses? Will we be the fathers who set a new standard for what it means to be a man of God? "I have given you the choice between life and death, between blessings and curses. Now I call on heaven and earth to witness the choice you make. Oh, that you would choose life, so that you and your descendants might live!" – Deuteronomy 30:19 (NLT) The future of fatherhood is in our hands.

The Generational Shift: Breaking Curses, Building Legacies

For too long, fatherhood has been under attack. Generations of men grew up without fathers. Many carried the wounds of absent or abusive fathers. Cycles of dysfunction, neglect, and trauma have been passed down. But now, it stops with us. We will be the fathers who break the chains of the past. We will be the men who stand in the gap for our children. We will be the generation that restores the honor of fatherhood. "But the love of the Lord remains forever with those who fear him. His salvation extends to the children's children of those who are faithful to his covenant, of those who obey his commandments!" – Psalm 103:17-18 (NLT)

Hard Times Create Strong Fathers, Strong Fathers Create Strong Families

There is a quote that says: "Hard times create strong men. Strong men create good times. Good times create weak men. Weak men create hard times." This applies directly to fatherhood. Weak fatherhood leads to broken families. Broken families lead to lost children. Lost children grow into weak men who repeat the cycle. We are now at a turning point in history. We must be the strong fathers who create strong families. We must raise sons who know discipline, strength, and honor. We must raise daughters who know love, protection, and self-worth. The easy road leads to destruction, but the hard road leads to legacy. "The diligent make good plans and work hard; their efforts bring profit. But those who are too lazy to work are soon poor." – Proverbs 21:5 (NLT) We are the fathers who must choose the hard path—the path of discipline, wisdom,

73

and leadership. The future of fatherhood depends on it.

A Vision for the Future: What the Next Generation Needs

The future doesn't change by accident—it changes through intentional action. If we want our sons and daughters to walk in righteousness, wisdom, and strength, we must: Teach them what it means to be a man and woman of God. Show them through our actions, not just our words. Raise them in truth, discipline, and love. The next generation needs us to be fathers who are: God-centered – Fathers who pray, seek wisdom, and lead their homes with faith. Present and engaged – Fathers who are emotionally, mentally, and physically present. Builders of generational wealth – Fathers who teach financial wisdom and responsibility. Warriors against deception – Fathers who protect their children from lies, temptations, and negative influences. Role models of righteousness – Fathers who set the standard for integrity, honor, and character.

Building a World Where Fatherhood Thrives

The future of fatherhood is not just about what we do in our homes—it is about how we influence the world. We must: Raise our voices in our communities – Advocating for strong families and father-friendly policies. Mentor the next generation of young men – Teaching them what true manhood looks like. Hold other fathers accountable – Encouraging, sharpening, and supporting one another. Challenge the media and culture – Rejecting false portrayals of men and fathers. Restore respect for marriage and family – Upholding God's design for fatherhood. "They will be called oaks of righteousness, a planting of the Lord for the display of his splendor." – Isaiah 61:3 (NLT) This isn't just about us—it is about the world our children will inherit. If we want strong families, thriving communities, and a restored society, it starts with strong fathers.

The Final Charge: Fathers, Our Mission Is Clear

We are not just raising children—we are raising the next generation of leaders. We are not just protecting our homes—we are shaping the future of society. We are not just fighting for our families—we are fighting for righteousness. The future of fatherhood starts with you. Your leadership matters. Your presence matters. Your love, your wisdom, your discipline—IT ALL MATTERS.

The Father's Final Prayer for the Future

"Heavenly Father, I pray for the future of fatherhood in this world. Raise up men who will stand in righteousness. Strengthen the fathers who feel weak. Heal the wounds of those who have been broken. Let every child know the love of a present, godly father. Break the chains of generational curses, and release the blessing of wisdom, love, and strength. Let our sons walk in integrity. Let our daughters know their worth. Let our homes be filled with Your presence. Father, we commit our lives to shaping the future. In Yahshua's (Jesus') name, Amen."

Final Reflection: The Legacy We Leave Behind

One day, our time here will be done. Our names will fade from the records of history. Our achievements will be forgotten by the world. But the impact we made as fathers will live on. The way we raised our children... The values we instilled... The love, wisdom, and faith we passed down... That is our true legacy. That is how we change the world.

The Last Words of This Book: Rise Up and Lead

Fathers, this is your time. Do not wait. Do not hesitate. Do not doubt. You were called, chosen, and equipped for this moment. Now, rise up and lead. "For the Lord your God is with you wherever you go." – Joshua 1:9 (NLT)

The Invitation to Salvation

A Call to Surrender Your Life to Christ

If something in this book awakened your spirit, it's not by chance—it's a divine invitation. God is calling you to Himself, and the door is open.

You can begin your journey with a simple, sincere prayer:

"Lord Yahshua (Jesus), I believe You died for my sins and rose again so I could have new life. I surrender my life to You. Come into my heart, forgive me, and lead me into Your truth. Today, I choose to follow You. Amen."

If you prayed that prayer, welcome to the family of God. Heaven rejoices with you. Now walk in your purpose and power.

Books from Kingdom Legacy Press

- The Method Man
- The Power of a Praying Man
- The Power of a Praying Athlete
- The Power of a Praying Coach
- Rooted in Goodness
- Fathers Matter

- God's Timing is Perfect Timing
- Fixing Me, Not Him
- They'll Thank You Later
- You Are Never Too Broken

Stay Connected & Grow

Visit www.KingdomLegacyPress.com to subscribe for devotionals, online studies, and upcoming book releases.

You can also find resources to help deepen your faith, strengthen your family, and live a life aligned with God.

Join the movement. Walk in purpose. Become the light.

www.ingramcontent.com/pod-product-compliance
Lightning Source LLC
Chambersburg PA
CBHW071113120626
46546CB00003B/1319